Vintage Humor for Wine Lovers

Written and
compiled by
Malcolm Kushner, AFHC

**Malcolm Kushner
& Associates**

Malcolm Kushner & Associates
P.O. Box 7509
Santa Cruz, CA 95061
Tel: 831-425-4839
Fax: 831-451-9451
Email: mk@kushnergroup.com
http:www.kushnergroup.com

Design: Rachael Brune rbrune@canyondesign.com
Illustrations: John Claude Hundt jchundt@aol.com
Editor: Christine Griger
Cover Photo: Licensed from Corbis

Library of Congress Control Number: 2002112666

For Sam,
you are the sonshine of my life.

TABLE OF CONTENTS

Introduction

"THE CLINK OF GLASSES FILLED with wine sounds empty without laughter." Famous words from an old poet? Nah. I just made it up. But it does epitomize the philosophy of this book – that your experience of wine can be greatly enriched by humor.

Just for a moment abandon your search for the perfect pairing of wine and food. This traditional obsession has long obscured other considerations that have as much, or more, to do with wine appreciation. Sparkling conversation. Intimate communication. Developing a genuine rapport with your companions. These factors, which are all facilitated by humor, greatly affect your enjoyment of wine. So ease up on what wine goes with what food. A better question is what wine goes with what joke?

A shaggy dog story with a glass of sherry? A topical monologue with a bottle of Beaujolais? A one-line zinger with a decanter of Zinfandel? It's your choice. There are no rules. (Except for fish stories—they don't go with red wine.)

When properly selected, a combination of wit and wine can be extraordinary. There's nothing quite comparable to the sound of a chuckle as a vintage year passes lazily across your tastebuds. (Well, almost nothing.) The interplay of the senses is pure ecstasy. Ever notice that the word 'delicious' applies to both wit and wine? It's not a coincidence.

How can you maximize the intoxicating experience of wit and wine? Just read this book. It's full of quotes, jokes, cartoons and anecdotes guaranteed to turn wine lovers into wine laughers. What humor should you choose? Anything that's funny to you and your companions will work.

Of course, different people find different things funny. Or, as the saying goes, there's no accounting for taste. (How else can you explain The Brady Bunch?) But don't despair. I've anticipated the problem. That's why this book contains humor on so many aspects of wine. From tasting and toasting to insults and inebriation, you'll find something for everyone—even teetotalers.

British social reformer Lady Astor once announced, "I would rather commit adultery than drink a glass of beer." Immediately, a voice from the crowd yelled, "Who wouldn't?" I doubt they felt the same way about wine.

Salute. Cheers. L'Chaim.

Malcolm Kushner
Santa Cruz, California
November 2002

Chapter 1

QUE SYRAH SYRAH

WILLIAM SOKOLIN ONCE ASKED, "What is the definition of a good wine?" And he answered, "It should start and end with a smile." Why did Sokolin answer his own question? Who knows? Maybe it was rhetorical. Or maybe he was drunk at the time. In either case, he was onto something. Wine should start and end with a smile. And there should be lots of laughter in between.

Of course many besides Sokolin have offered definitions of wine. Margaret Fuller called it "the earth's answer to the sun." Marilyn Clark called it "music from the vineyard." Clifton Fadiman called it "the soul of good living." And Werumeus Buning called wine "the flower in the buttonhole of civilization."

I like to think of it as the squirting flower in the buttonhole of civilization. Because wine should be fun. Not exactly wine by the Groucho glasses. But fun.

In this chapter, you will be immersed in some fun, and funnier, aspects of wine. As Woody Allen has noted, man does not kill only for food, "frequently there must be a beverage."

"A meal without wine is like a day without sunshine, except that on a day without sunshine you can still get drunk."

Lee Entrekin

"I cook with wine, sometimes I even add it to the food!"

Leslie Duncan

"On one occasion someone put a very little wine into a glass, and said that it was sixteen years old. 'It is very small for its age,' said Gnathaena."

Athenaeus

"If all the vine rows in Australia were laid end to end, they would reach nearly to the moon...but how would we pick the grapes?"

John Wilson

"I'm so holy that when I drink wine, it turns into water."

Aga Kan III

"I made wine out of raisins so I wouldn't have to wait for it to age."

Steven Wright

THOUGHTS ON WINE

"My idea of a fine wine was one that merely stained your teeth without stripping the enamel."

Clive James

"I shall drink no wine before it is time! OK, it is time."

Groucho Marx

"The fine wine leaves you with something pleasant; the ordinary wine just leaves."

Maynard Amerine

"Winemaking is the world's second oldest profession, and, no doubt, it has eased the burden of the world's oldest."

Tony Aspler

"Wine is the reason I get up every afternoon."

Anonymous

"People do not age as well as wine because meat spoils faster than grapes do."

Nettie

"That which belongs to another."

Diogenes, when asked what wine he liked to drink

EVERYTHING I NEED TO KNOW I LEARNED FROM DRINKING WINE

You can account for taste — some people don't have any.

·

There's a big difference between old and aged.

·

Even crap sounds delicious in French.

·

Room temperature depends on the room.

·

Never give a corkscrew to a drunk.

·

Price isn't everything.

·

Whether the glass is half empty or half full depends on what's in it.

·

Plastic cups are for urine samples.

EVERYTHING I NEED TO KNOW I LEARNED FROM DRINKING WINE

An expert is someone who read the label when you weren't looking.

•

Don't cry over spilled milk — wine, on the other hand, stains.

•

A loaded person can be more dangerous than a loaded gun.

•

When something is the specialty of the house, ask whose house.

•

A regurgitated beverage doesn't go with anything.

•

When life stinks put a cork in it.

A wine tasting group that met once a month acquired a reputation for its wild meetings. A police officer who heard about it decided to arrest whoever left the meeting the drunkest. After setting up surveillance across the street from where the wine tasters met, he waited.

The first guy to come out fell down the stairs, got up and walked into a tree, got up again and fumbled for his car keys. The second person to come out also seemed a bit tipsy, but the cop decided to wait for the first guy, who was now looking for his car by trying his keys in every car in the parking lot.

Soon all of the people at the wine tasting meeting had gotten into their respective cars and driven off. The only man left was the dead drunk that the cop was waiting for. The man finally got into the only car left in the lot and after fumbling with his keys, got the car started. That's when the cop pulled in behind the man's car and and began to arrest him.

The man insisted on a breathalyzer test, so the cop tested him on the spot. To the cop's amazement, the man had a zero % blood alcohol level. The cop couldn't believe it. He asked the man why he appeared so drunk.

The man replied, "I'm the designated decoy."

"Sometimes too much to drink isn't enough."

Unknown

"A truly great wine should not leave you with a foam mustache."

Lister

"A small carafe of wine is illogical, immoral, and inadequate."

Unknown

"Tomorrow never comes, but the morning after certainly does."

Unknown

"If drinking interferes with your job, quit your job."

Unknown

"If you drink enough wine, it doesn't matter how bad it is."

Unknown

"Wine improves with age. The older I get, the better I like it."

Unknown

"The road to great wine is littered with beer bottles."

Unknown

"Reality is an illusion created by alcohol deficiency."

Unknown

Q & A ABOUT WINE

Q. *How do you make a small fortune in the wine business?*

A. Start with a large fortune and buy a winery.

Q. *What's the difference between God and a wine critic?*

A. God doesn't think He's a wine critic!

Q. *When should you drink a really good wine?*

A. As often as possible.

Q. *How can you tell a bunch of wine snobs from
a bunch of grapes?*

A. Jump up and down on them. If you get wine,
you've got grapes!

Q. *Who invented the first champagne with no bubbles?*

A. Dumb Perignon

Q. *Did you hear about the new tasting room on the moon?*

A. Great wine but no atmosphere.

Q. *If a wine critic says something in the forest and no one hears him is he still pompous?*

A. Yes.

Q. *What would you call a pretentious know-it-all who works at an upholstery shop?*

A. A recovering wine critic.

"It's a full-bodied wine with hints of acrimony, partisanship, and moral outrage."

A preacher was completing a temperance sermon. With great expression he said, "If I had all the red wine in the world, I'd take it and throw it into the river."

With even greater emphasis he said, "And if I had all the white wine in the world, I'd take it and throw it into the river."

And finally he said, "And if I had all the champagne in the world, I'd take it and throw it into the river." He sat down.

The song leader then stood very cautiously and announced with a smile, "For our closing song, let us sing Hymn # 365: 'Shall We Gather at the River'."

1. You know what wine goes with a cherry popsicle.

2. You didn't know champagne is a color.

3. You check the vintage of bottled water.

4. You can't pass a cork bulletin board without sniffing it.

5. You say things like 'a pungent yet tranquil insouciance' when talking about orange juice.

6. You never realized that bouquet has anything to do with flowers.

7. You think a 'nose job' means changing a wine's aroma.

8. Your idea of a power tool is a battery-operated corkscrew.

Chapter 2

PUT A CORK IN IT

JOHN ROMANO ONCE SAID, "The smaller the understanding of the situation, the more pretentious the form of expression." I'm not sure what situation he was referring to, but his observation certainly applies to the world of wine. From snooty waiters to pompous tasters to arrogant experts, wine aficionados can sometimes be a condescending bunch.

Writer John Updike has noted that, "A healthy male adult bore consumes each year one and a half times his own weight in other people's patience." By extrapolation, I'd say that a healthy adult of either gender who claims to know about wine consumes several times their weight in other people's patience. Too often, they're all decanter and no beverage.

Haven't you ever wanted to tell them to just put a cork in it? In this chapter that's exactly what you'll learn how to do. Comebacks to snotty questions and remarks. Reverse intimidation. Counter-pretentiousness moves. You'll never be caught flat again. (And you'll know how to berate a waiter if your champagne is.)

Verbal aggression isn't your style? No problem. Just heed the advice of Herm Albright who said, "A positive attitude may not solve all your problems, but it will annoy enough people to make it worth the effort."

Shakespeare said we weave a tangled web when we deceive. And your parents told you honesty is the best policy. But sometimes, gosh darn it, you just have to lie. Well not lie exactly—fake it. And many of those times involve interacting with obnoxious wine know-it-alls at parties, dinners and similar events. Yes, you could just admit that you don't know much about wine —and certainly less than these self-proclaimed experts do. But why give them the satisfaction? Instead, when asked to comment, use one of these all-purpose lines.

You Want to be Generally Dismissive

"It has great typicity."

"It has legs, but no ankle."

"An irritating little wine, but probably unavoidable."

"This wine is almost Congressional in its predictability."

"It's not a wine that commands your attention, but rather, abuses it."

You Want to Upset the Wine Provider

"I don't know...I think it might be a little corked."

You Want to Insult the Expert

"It has a nutty taste...with a deep odor. Not unlike your armpit."

You Won't Play the Game

"This tastes just like wine."

You Turn the Game Around

"This wine reminds me of _____.
(Fill in a complex subject on which you're an expert and the wine snob is not.)

For example: This wine reminds me of a Federal Communications Commission ruling on bandwidth auctions.

You've gone to a bar to relax, contemplate your life and drink a glass of wine. You're sitting deep in thought when the inevitable occurs — some bore tries to pick you up. Here are some answers you can give when you're on the receiving end of common pickup lines.

Will you join me in a glass of wine? *I don't think there'd be room for both of us.*

Have you ever tried drinking Australian wine? *What else would I be doing with it?*

Can I buy you a glass of wine? *I'd rather just have the cash.*

Stay a minute and let me get you a glass of wine. *Just give me the cash - I'll get one later.*

Would you like another glass of wine? *Do you really think our relationship will last that long?*

What would you say if I asked if I could buy you a glass of wine? *Nothing. I can't talk and laugh at the same time.*

What do you think of the wine here? *Better than the company.*

Didn't we meet in a past life? *Yes, and I wouldn't let you buy me a glass of wine then, either.*

Helmut Schonwalder is a legendary waiter and creator of The Waiter's Digest — a web site devoted to hospitality skills. The range of advice and information provided on the site is extraordinary. It even includes what to do if you accidentally spill wine when opening a bottle.

The suggested solution is one that Helmut devised when he had the misfortune to open a bottle incorrectly. After the cork popped out, a stream of wine landed on the floor. Instead of apologizing, he made the mistake seem part of the act. How? He regaled his customers with a story about the 'charming Roman custom of spilling wine before dinner.' He explained that it was a little known ancient Italian ritual designed to please the gods and bring good luck and fortune.

Yeah, right. If this happens to you, be ready to counterattack. Here are some potential responses:

"The ancient Romans also fed incompetent waiters to the lions."

"Does good luck and fortune mean we get a different waiter next time?"

"We follow an ancient Roman ritual too: no tip for baloney."

And here are some responses for other wine waiter goof-ups.

Your wine is served with bits of cork in it.
"I asked for wine, not cork soup."

The house wine tastes horrible.
"You said this was the house wine—whose house, the Adams Family?"

The waiter's fingerprints are inside your glass.
"The FBI can't use this unless your fingerprints are on the outside."

WINE WAITER FULL DECKISMS

The expression 'not playing with a full deck' describes a person who makes a mental effort of less than 100% — usually a lot less. Many variations on this theme have evolved over the last several years. And they've been applied to a wide array of occupations. Here are a few to describe the mental state of the next incompetent wine waiter you encounter.

A few pages short of a wine list.

A few grapes short of a bunch.

Less cultured than a yeast.

A few m's short of a sommelier.

All sparkle but no fizz.

The cork is in but nobody's home.

A few years short of a good vintage.

The cork is out but nobody's pouring.

A little moldy in the wine cellar.

Didn't crush all of his grapes.

WINE WAITER FULL DECKISMS

No wine in the bottle.

Playing wine steward without a corkscrew.

*When he was born they crushed a few too
many grapes.*

*Thinks he knows champagne because
he's a bubble-head.*

Not the biggest cluster in the vineyard.

Too much air in his fermenter.

Not enough oak in the barrel.

They harvested his grapes a little too soon.

His IQ is an ideal serving temperature.

BIGGEST LIES ABOUT WINE

1. Oh that's just a bit of cork.

2. The French love this one.

3. That was a good year.

4. It goes with anything.

5. It's a steal at this price.

"eBay '99."

CLUES THAT A RESTAURANT DOESN'T SPECIALIZE IN WINE

1. Wine glasses are plastic.

2. Half bottles featured on wine list have jagged edges.

3. Wine list features
   (1.) Red
   (2.) White
   (3.) Rosé

   and asks you to order by number.

4. You can take home what's left in the box.

5. White wines are pre-chilled with ice cubes.

6. Wine dispensed by vending machine.

7. After opening wine, waiter sniffs bottle and says it's OK.

8. Michelin Guide rates it in tires instead of stars.

Chapter 3

SPIN THE BOTTLE:
WINE, WOMEN AND SONG—AND MEN

SPIN THE BOTTLE:
WINE, WOMEN AND SONG—AND MEN

———————————•———————————

COMEDIAN HENNY YOUNGMAN once explained the secret of his long relationship with his wife. "We take time to go to a restaurant two times a week," he said. "A little candlelight, dinner, soft music and dancing. She goes Tuesdays, I go Fridays."

Whether or not you agree that absence makes the heart grow fonder, wine has always played an important role in romance. In fact, wine definitely makes the heart grow fonder—especially around closing time. H.L. Mencken once called love "the triumph of imagination over intelligence." Throughout history, much of that imagination has been fueled by wine.

In this chapter we will explore the relationship between men, women and wine. Can the language of love really be spoken in terms of merlots and beaujolais? Can a bottle of wine make up for a lot of mistakes? Can you have wining without dining?

And most important, can wine work the magic that brings two people together? Or as an old philosopher once observed, "They make a great couple; the rocks in her head fit the holes in his."

"Men are like fine wine. They all start out like grapes, and it's our job to stomp on them and keep them in the dark until they mature into something you'd like to have dinner with."

Anonymous

"Women are like fine wine. They all start out fresh, fruity and intoxicating to the mind and then turn full-bodied with age until they go all sour and vinegary and give you a headache."

Anonymous

"Drinking provides a beautiful excuse to pursue the one activity that truly gives me pleasure, hooking up with fat, hairy girls."

Ross Levy

"Sir, if you were my husband, I would poison your drink."

Lady Astor to Winston Churchill

"Madam, if you were my wife, I would drink it."

Winston Churchill

Woman: "Sir, you are drunk!"

Winston Churchill: "Indeed I am madam, but in the morning I shall be sober, whereas you shall still be ugly."

"There is no such thing as an ugly woman. Only too little wine."

Murphy's Laws on Sex

"I told my wife that a husband is like a fine wine; he gets better with age. The next day, she locked me in the cellar."

Anonymous

"I spend nearly all my money on wine, women, and song – the rest, I waste."

Anonymous

"Platonic love is being invited into the wine cellar for a sip of pop."

Unknown

"A night without sex is like a meal without wine. A meal without sex is like a night without wine. A meal without wine is like a night without sex. Sex without wine can still be pretty good."

Anonymous

"Compromises are for relationships, not wine."

Sir Robert Scott Caywood

"In the order named these are the hardest to control: Wine, Women and Song."

Franklin P. Adams

"Wine is like sex in that few men will admit not knowing all about it."

Hugh Johnson

THE WINE VIRGIN

A woman was married several times to men in
the wine industry. Yet she remained a virgin.
How could that be? Here's her explanation.

My 1st husband was a wine-maker.
*He kept promising how good it was going to be if
we waited a few more years.*

My 2nd husband was a wine critic.
He just wanted to talk about it.

My 3rd husband was a professional wine taster.
All he wanted to do was — well, you know.

My 4th husband was a wine collector.
He just wanted to look at it.

My 5th husband was a winery accountant.
He was only interested in the bottom line.

My 6th husband was a wine marketer.
*He had a nice product but he never knew how to
position it.*

My 7th husband was a grape grower.
He just wanted to stomp on me.

WHY CHAMPAGNE IS BETTER THAN A MAN

1. Champagne containers are never barrel shaped.

2. Champagne improves with age.

3. An empty champagne bottle can be made into a table lamp.

4. Champagne is always sparkling.

5. Champagne quietly fizzes and doesn't snore.

6. Champagne will wait patiently while you dress and do your hair.

7. Champagne gives you a headache afterwards—not before.

8. You don't have to boost its ego.

9. Champagne doesn't run out of clean underwear.

10, Champagne never falls asleep in front of the TV.

A TOUGH DECISION

German poet Johann Wolfgang Goethe was once asked which three things he would take to an island. He stated: "Poetry, a beautiful woman and enough bottles of the world's finest wines to survive this dry period!"

Then he was asked what he would leave back first, if he could only take only two things. And he replied: "The poetry!"

Slightly surprised, the man asked the next question: "And Sir, what would you leave back if only one was allowed?" Goethe thought for a couple of minutes and answered: "It depends on the vintage!"

A playboy looking for action picked-up a beautiful woman at a wine bar. After offering to buy her a drink, he asked whether she preferred sherry or port. "Oh, sherry by all means!" she replied.

"Sherry is like the nectar of the gods. Just looking at it in a crystal-like decanter fills me with the anticipation of a heavenly thrill. When the stopper is removed and the beautiful liquid is poured into the glass and I inhale the delicious tangy aroma, I'm lifted on the wings of ecstasy. As I taste the magic potion, my whole being thrills and glows, it seems like a thousand violins throb in my ears, I'm carried into another world and I just want to make love."

Trembling with excitement, the playboy asked "What happens when you drink port?" The woman replied, "I belch."

WHAT GOES WITH WINE

A popular class among Cornell University seniors is 'Introduction to Wines,' a course in which students learn correct pairings of wine and food. After sampling some German wines, the professor pointed to a male enrollee and asked, "What do you think would go well with this Riesling?" He paused, then replied, "A date."

GOOD COMMUNICATION

One night, a guy walked into a bar and asked the bartender for a glass of wine. Then he asked for another. After a couple more glasses, the bartender got worried. "What's the matter?" the bartender asked. "My wife and I got into a fight," explained the guy, "and she vowed not to talk to me for 31 days . . ." He downed another glass, and said, "And tonight is the last night."

A man and a woman get into a bad car accident. Both cars are totally demolished. But amazingly neither the man or the woman is hurt. After they crawl out of their cars, the woman says, "Wow! Just look at our cars. There's nothing left. I can't believe we're alive. This must be a sign from God that we should meet and be friends." The man replies, "I agree with you completely; this must be a sign from God!"

The woman continues, "And look at this – here's another miracle. My car is completely demolished but this bottle of wine didn't break. Surely God wants us to drink this wine and celebrate our good fortune."

Then she hands the bottle to the man. The man nods in agreement, opens the bottle, takes a few big swigs, then hands it back to the woman. The woman takes the bottle and immediately hands it back to the man. The man asks, "Aren't you having any?" The woman replies, "No. I think I'll just wait for the police."

A man walks into a bar and orders a glass of wine. Then he looks into his shirt pocket and orders another glass of wine. After he finishes, he looks into his shirt pocket again and orders another glass of wine. The bartender is curious and asks him, "Every time you order a glass of wine, you look in your shirt pocket. Why?" The man replies, "I have a picture of my wife in my pocket and when she starts to look good, I go home."

COULDN'T MAKE IT

A wine aficionado trying to get tickets to a famous annual lecture by the world's top wine critics finally obtained a couple of seats a year in advance.

When the exciting night arrived, the woman in front of the wine aficionado noticed the seat next to him was empty. So she asked him why such a valuable commodity was unused. He said that his wife couldn't make it. The woman asked him if he didn't have any friends or relatives who could have used the seat. He replied, "No. They're all at her funeral."

A prominent female executive returns home after a conference in Paris. As she steps off the Concorde at Kennedy Airport her waiting assistant notices that she is carrying a case of Chateau Petrus 1990.

"Nice wine," says the assistant. "Thanks! I got it for my husband!" responds the executive. The assistant pauses for a second, then nodding her head enthusiastically, says: "Good trade!"

"That will be perfect. We have a lot to talk about."

Chapter 4

VENI, VIDI, VINO:
I CAME, I SAW, I GOT DRUNK

VENI, VIDI, VINO:
I CAME, I SAW, I GOT DRUNK

———————•———————

AUTHOR G.K. CHESTERTON once said, "No animal ever invented anything as bad as drunkenness — or as good as drink." But animal inventors aside, inebriation has always been one of the major purposes for drinking wine. (Or getting others to drink it.) Writer Ambrose Bierce succinctly described this timeless quest for intoxication in his definition of Bacchus, the Roman god of wine: "A convenient deity invented by the ancients as an excuse for getting drunk."

Throughout the ages, drinking wine and getting drunk have gone hand-in-hand. For example, in 19th century France, Louis Pasteur observed, "A bottle of wine contains more philosophy than all the books in the world." And you know, he must have been pretty tanked up when he said that.

In this chapter, you will find humorous items related to imbibing too much of the fruit of the vine. This includes warning signs of intoxication, as well as ways to measure your degree of inebriation and philosophical observations about over-indulging. But don't let such talk get in the way of a good bender. Just remember the immortal words of Homer Simpson: "It's not whether you win or lose — it's how drunk you get."

———————

OBSERVATIONS ABOUT INEBRIATION

"You're not drunk if you can lie on the floor without holding on."

Dean Martin

"Bartender, I'd like whatever the man on the floor was drinking."

Unknown

"The hard part about being a bartender is figuring out who is drunk and who is just stupid."

Richard Braunstein

"Karaoke bars combine two of the nation's greatest evils: people who shouldn't drink with people who shouldn't sing."

Tom Dreesen

"Be wary of strong drink. It can make you shoot at tax collectors and miss."

Lazarus Long

"Every time I learn something new it pushes some old stuff out of my brain. Like that time I took that home wine-making course and forgot how to drive."

Homer Simpson

"March is the month God created to show people who don't drink what a hangover is like."

Garrison Keillor

"Life is a waste of time, time is a waste of life, so get wasted all of the time and have the time of your life."

Michelle Mastrolacasa

"I got so wasted one night I waited for the Stop sign to change, and it did."

Steve Krabitz

"Alcohol is a very necessary article. It enables Parliament to do things at eleven at night that no sane person would do at eleven in the morning."

George Bernard Shaw

"I'd rather have a bottle in front of me than a frontal lobotomy."

Tom Waits

"I've taken more out of alcohol than alcohol has ever taken from me."

Sir Winston Churchill

"I have never been drunk. On occasion, I may have been over-served."

Unknown

"I was so drunk last night, I fell down and missed the floor."

Dean Martin

"My uncle was the town drunk and we lived in Chicago."

George Gobel

"I told my girlfriend last night how much I loved her, and she said that I must have been out drinking again. I asked her why she would say that, and she said, 'Because I'm your father'."

Dave George

"There's too much blood in my alcohol system."

Anonymous

OBSERVATIONS ABOUT INEBRIATION

"Going to the opera, like getting drunk, is a sin that carries its own punishment with it."

Hannah More

"Drunk is feeling sophisticated when you can't say it."

Anonymous

"You are not drunk if you lie under the table. When you no longer order from there, then you are drunk."

Unknown

"Abstainer: a weak person who yields to the temptation of denying himself a pleasure."

Ambrose Bierce

"The problem with some people is that when they aren't drunk, they're sober."

William Butler Yeats

SIX SIGNS YOU'VE HAD TOO MUCH

1. Drinking out of a shoe — and it's not yours.

2. Sniffing a cork that's still in the bottle.

3. Swirling wine while it's still in the bottle.

4. Asking if there's a movie version of the wine list.

5. When someone is injured opening a wine bottle you scream "Is there a sommelier in the house?"

7. Thinking you can sell a wine bottle full of sediment as a snow globe.

"Haven't you ever seen California wine being made before?"

NEW WINE WARNING LABELS

In a continuing quest to enhance the health of its citizens, the government may impose new label warning requirements on wine makers. Here are some of the warnings under consideration.

WARNING:

Consumption of alcohol may cause you to lose arguments with inanimate objects.

WARNING:

Consumption of alcohol may cause the back of your head to get hit by a toilet seat.

WARNING:

Consumption of alcohol may cause David Lynch films to make sense.

WARNING:

Consumption of alcohol may cause politicians to appear intelligent.

WARNING:

Consumption of alcohol may cause you to wake up naked in a bus depot.

NEW WINE WARNING LABELS

WARNING:

Consumption of alcohol may cause you to mistake
dirty laundry for breakfast.

WARNING:

Consumption of alcohol may make you fail to notice
that the toilet lid is down when you sit on it.

WARNING:

Consumption of alcohol may cause you to write
speeches for Marcel Marceau.

WARNING:

Consumption of alcohol may cause you to create a
Broadway show out of ABBA music.

TASTING ROOM TROUBLE
SHOOTING GUIDE

SYMPTOM: Drinking fails to give taste and satisfaction, wine is unusually pale & clear.
FAULT: Glass empty.
ACTION: Ask tasting room attendant for a wine sample.

SYMPTOM: Floor blurred.
FAULT: You are looking through bottom of empty glass.
ACTION: Ask to sample another wine.

SYMPTOM: Everything has gone dim, mouth full of cheese & crackers.
FAULT: You have fallen forward onto the tasting room bar.
ACTION: Ask for a wine that goes with crumbs.

SYMPTOM: Floor moving.
FAULT: You are being carried out.
ACTION: Find out if you are being taken to another winery.

SYMPTOM: Everything has gone dark.
FAULT: The winery is closing.
ACTION: Act like you would have bought something if they'd only stayed open a little longer.

SYMPTOM: You awaken to find your bed hard, cold and wet. You cannot see your bedroom.
FAULT: You have spent the night in the winery parking lot.
ACTION: Find out what time the winery opens.

JUGGLING ACT

A juggler, driving to his next performance, was stopped by the police. "Why are those knives in your car?" asked an officer. "I juggle them in my act," explained the juggler.

"Oh yeah?" says the cop. "Let's see you do it." So the juggler starts tossing and juggling the knives. Just then an elderly couple drives by and sees all this. "Wow, I'm glad I quit drinking," says the old man to his wife. "Look at the test they make you do now!"

EXCUSES

A police officer pulls over a driver who's been weaving in and out of lanes. He goes up to the driver's window and says, "Sir, I need you to blow into this breathalyzer tube." The man says, "Sorry, officer, I can't do that."

The cop asks, "Why not?" The driver says, "I'm an asthmatic and I'll have a really bad asthma attack."

The cop says, "Then you'll have to come down to the station to give a blood sample." "I can't do that either," says the driver. The cop asks, "Why not?"

The driver says, "I'm a hemophiliac and I'll bleed to death." "OK," says the officer, "then you'll have to give a urine sample."

"Sorry, I can't,"says the driver. The cop asks, "Why not?"

The driver says, "I'm also a diabetic and with a urine test I'll get really low blood sugar." So the cop says, "Then get out of the car and walk this white line."

The driver says, "I can't do that either." The cop asks, "Why not?" The driver says, "Because I'm drunk."

A man walks into a wine bar and orders five glasses of wine. The bartender is surprised because the man is alone, but he serves him the five glasses. The man drinks them one right after the other. Then he orders four more glasses of wine. The bartender serves him and the man drinks them right down again. Then the man orders three glasses and drinks them right down.

Then he orders one glass of wine. The bartender puts it down in front of him. And the man stares at the glass trying to focus.

Then he says to the bartender, "Y'know, it'sh a funny t'ing, but the less I drink, the drunker I get."

After spending a happy evening toasting each other in a wine bar, two friends promised to meet again in ten years at the same bar, same time. Ten years later, the first one walks in, looks around, and sure enough, there is his friend on a bar stool. He clasps the old friend's hand and cries, "The day we left, I didn't think I'd really see you here!" The friend looks up, stares, sways slightly and asks, "Who left?"

DRUNK TEST

Forget the breathalyzer. Here's a simple test that doesn't require special equipment to determine how drunk you are. Just answer each question honestly and see how you score.

QUESTIONS

1. A pair of twins enters the bar. When you look at them you see:
   a. Two people
   b. Four people
   c. Nothing—because you can't open your eyes

2. You light a match and blow on it. The match will:
   a. Go out
   b. Flare up
   c. Start a 3-alarm fire

3. You look up at the TV over the bar. A re-run of 'Gilligan's Island' is playing. You think it's:

   a. Mildly amusing
   b. The funniest thing you've ever seen
   c. Really meaningful

4. Despite your best efforts, you can't pick up
   a. A waiter
   b. A bartender
   c. A chair

5. How will you leave the bar?
   a. Walk out
   b. Stumble out
   c. Carried out

SCORING

0 points	For each question answered a.
10 points	For each question answered b.
25 points	For each question answered c.
1,000 points	For each question answered d.

WHAT IT MEANS

0 points	You just arrived at the bar or you're the designated driver.
10 points	Murphy's Law of Drinking applies to you: the best way to prevent a hangover is to stay drunk
25 points	You can't say 'no' to booze because you're unconscious.
1,000 points	You are now officially a toxic waste site.

Chapter 5

PARDON MY FRENCH

———————————•———————————

JOHANN WOLFGANG VON GOETHE once said, "Mathematicians are like Frenchmen: whatever you say to them they translate into their own language, and forthwith it is something entirely different." I don't know about mathematicians,but he was right about the French – especially when it comes to wine.

Learning to speak about wine isn't easy. It's as tough as learning a foreign language – and for good reason. There are lots of words and phrases you've never heard before. Many of them are in French. And many seem to make no sense at all. (Often the ones in French.)

Don't worry. In this chapter, you'll learn how to break the code. You'll be spewing French wine-speak in no time. And even if it doesn't mean anything, it will sound impressive. As Steven King observed, "French is the language that turns dirt into romance." Or, as we like to say back at the winebar, corked swill into vin magnifique.

And remember, if you have trouble faking the French just follow the advice of legendary politician Sam Rayburn. He said, "No one has a finer command of language than the person who keeps his mouth shut."

In California's Sonoma Valley, where vineyards cater to wine snobbery, a woman phoned the classified ad department of a newspaper. She offered for sale what sounded like 'well-aged Caumcneur.' The ad taker was unfamiliar with that particular wine, but was used to the infusion of French words into the local vocabulary. "Could you please spell that?" she asked. "You know," said the woman impatiently, 'c o-w - m-a-n-u r-e'."

A wine snob was at a tasting name-dropping all the rare, fancy bordeaux that he had tasted: Chateau Lafite, Latour, Mouton-Rothschild, etc. Tired of this, another guy opined, "well, my favorite bordeaux is Chateau Latose." "Latose?" said the snob, "I don't believe I'm familiar with that one." "You should be," said the other guy, "it's connected to Lafite!"

FRENCH ARMY KNIFE

FRENCH PRIMER FOR WINE STUDENTS

Avant-garde — opening a screw-top bottle with a corkscrew

Beret — device used to cover face when buying cheap wine

Blanc — color your face turns when you see the bill

Cru — friends you go drinking with

Cul-de-sac — putting cheap wine in a brown paper bag

Déjà vu — to see a wine again after you've already consumed it (see Regurgitation)

D'un certain âge — a number of years that is celebrated for wine and concealed for women

Esprit de corps — getting drunk with a bunch of people

Faux Pas — offering to pay your brother-in-law's wine tab

Femme fatale — a woman who drinks more than your credit card limit

FRENCH PRIMER FOR WINE STUDENTS

Finesse — Getting someone else to pay

Gauche — spilling red wine on fish

Hors d'oeuvre — a small piece of food used as an excuse to drink a big glass of wine

Je ne sais quoi — something is floating in the wine and it's not a piece of cork
Usage: *This has that je ne sais quoi.*

Maitre d' — restaurant supervisor who makes sure wine is properly aged by delaying your entrance

Magnifique — Word you say when tasting the swill your brother-in-law gave you for Christmas

Menu a clef — Wine list where the names have been changed to protect the guilty

Nouveau — type of money possessed by people who obsess over wine

Par excellence — drinking good wine at a golf course

Pièce de résistance — a cork

Rouge — Color your face turns when you see your brother-in-law's wine tab (See *Faux Pas*)

Savoir faire — knowing how to make a sommelier feel humble

Sur lie — Attitude of many sommeliers

"Is Pinot Noir where you want to be?"

WINE WORDS THAT SHOULD EXIST BUT DON'T

Despite the extensive vocabulary already associated with wine, there are many situations that still cry out for description by a single word or phrase. Here are some suggestions for correcting this problem.

Blendonomics—economics of producing cheap wines

Bottlefarm — an amateur wine cellar

Caskew — a wine casket that's tilted to one side

Caroma — smell of wine left in an automobile

Cellarceny — price of wine in a fancy restaurant

Chardonaysal — wine that comes out someone's nose

Compositioned — to be discovered putting cheap wine in an expensive bottle

Corkivore — a person who drinks wine with pieces of cork in it

Corkscrewed — treatment by snotty wine steward or sommelier

Crushware — feet

WINE WORDS THAT SHOULD EXIST BUT DON'T

Decantaloupe – to transfer wine from a bottle to a fruit

Drinkblot Test – device to assess the sanity of inebriates

Drinkling to perceive a tiny bit of reality through an alcoholic fog

Exhaust Fume-Blanc – see Caroma

Extractuary – professional who estimates the cost of opening a wine bottle incorrectly

Fermental Case – wine nut

Grapex – grape that's at the top of its form.

Imbribe – to pay off a law enforcement official who finds you inebriated

Noble Rote – memorized wine facts recited in attempt to impress companions

Nuancentric – obsessed with the slightest hints of flavor in wine

Oenologisticulate – when a wine expert gives you the middle finger

WINE WORDS THAT SHOULD EXIST BUT DON'T

Oxidazed — describes a person who has drunk too much wine that has been exposed to air.

Robusted — apprehended by law enforcement while drinking intense, full-bodied wine

Sedimention — to speak endlessly about a speck floating in the bottle

Taint necessarily so — disagreement about acceptability of just opened bottle of wine

Tannincompoop — a person who babbles incessantly about a wine's tannin content

Vintagious — pompous attitude about wine that spreads from one person to another.

Vintnervous — to worry that wine comes from a non-prestigious winery

Weinstine — big expert on wine

Wine / whine situation — customer argument with wine steward in which both parties lose

Zinfandeli — any cheap wine bought at the corner store

Chapter 6

TASTING...1...2...3

GEORGE BERNARD SHAW ONCE SAID, "Do not do unto others as you would they should do unto you. Their tastes may not be the same." Isn't that the truth. And if you have any doubt, just accept your next invitation to a wine tasting. Opinions of a particular wine will range from hate to great. That's assuming you can understand what the tasters are talking about.

"A subtle yet annoying insouciance with a hint of uncannily herbaceous perfume." *Huh?*

"Deceptively mint and eucalyptus aromas precede a delicate flavor of dark berries on the palate without sacrificing some tasty sweet oak notes following onto a tidy little finish." *What?*

"An amusing little wine with the character of a Brady Bunch sibling and the texture of a pair of jeans on sale at Macy's." *Enough.*

In this chapter, you will learn the fun points (definitely not the fine points) of tasting, rating and punditizing about wine flavor. It's really not difficult. Just remember: half the wine in the world is below average. So you've got a 50-50 chance of being right. And if you're wrong, so what? As an old philosopher once said, "It's better to have poor taste than no taste at all."

"There are no dumb questions, only pretentious people."

Winegeek.com

"A good rule is to state that the bouquet is better than the taste and vice versa."

Stephen Potter

"If you want to become a rich, pretentious snot — and who doesn't? — you should learn about wine."

Dave Barry

"Wine experts are of two kinds, gastronomic and intellectual, distinguishable according to whether, on the sight of a bottle they reach for their glass or their glasses."

Thomas McKeown

"Can't we just get rid of wine lists? Do we really have to be reminded every time we go out to a nice restaurant that we have no idea what we are doing? Why don't they just give us a trigonometry quiz with the menu?"

Jerry Seinfeld

"This wine is particularly heavy, and is mostly recommended for hand-to-hand combat."

C. Hacking

"It's a naive wine without any breeding, but I think you'll be amused by its presumption."

James Thurber

"The wine seems to be very closed-in and seems to have entered a dumb stage. Sort of a Marcel Meursault."

Paul Winalski

A famous wine expert invited legendary composer Johannes Brahms to dinner. The wine expert then brought out some of his finest vintages. "This is the Brahms of my cellar," he said to his guests, producing a dust-covered bottle and pouring some into the master's glass.

Brahms looked first at the color of the wine, then sniffed its bouquet, finally took a sip, and put the glass down without saying a word. "Don't you like it?" asked the host. "Hmm," Brahms muttered. "Better bring your Beethoven!"

"So what do you think of it?"

A young professional on his first date with a stunning woman wanted to impress her with his knowledge of wine. "Bring a bottle of 1985 Sterling Chabernet Sauvignon from the Carneros District," he commanded the wine steward. Upon tasting the wine, the man complained, "This is a 1987 Vintage from the North Coast Vineyards near Calistoga. Now bring me what I ordered."

The steward fetched and poured another bottle of wine. Once again the man was upset. "This is 1985 all right, but it's from the Mount Helena vineyards!"

Watching the drama from the bar, an old drunk came up to the table and said, "Wow, that's an impressive ability. Can you tell me what's in my glass?"

Not wanting to pass up an opportunity to impress his date, the young professional sipped at the drunk's glass. "This tastes like urine!" he exclaimed and spat the mouthful out. "That's exactly right," said the drunk. "Now tell me when and where I was born."

SCORING WITH WINE

In the parlance of lowlifes, scoring some wine translates as acquiring wine — often by dubious means. In the parlance of wine aficionados, scoring some wine translates as assigning wine a numerical value — often by dubious means. There are probably as many wine-scoring systems as there are wines. They differ in numerical values, traits rated and underlying philosophy. But fear not. The following system is both easy to use and understand.

TO ADD POINTS

+10   You can't pronounce the name
+10   You'd buy it again
+10   Too good to give as a gift
+10   Not available at corner grocery store
+10   Financial planner recommends it
        as investment

TO SUBTRACT POINTS

-10   It comes in a box
-10   Pushing cork into bottle improves taste
-10   Pushing in screw-top improves taste
-10   Wouldn't even give as gift of cooking wine
-10   When opened, people ask, "Who cut one?"

SCORING		
	50	Will impress a wine snob
	10 to 40	Good stuff
	0	Hope the bottle is pretty
	-10 to -40	The Grateful Dead say you can share the women and the wine — not this wine!
	-50	Can double as paint remover

IF FAMOUS AUTHORS & COMEDIANS
WROTE ABOUT WINE

WILLIAM SHAKESPEARE ON FRENCH BURGUNDY

Much ado about nothing. Too saucy. Like a toad —
ugly and venomous. A very ancient and fish-like
smell. All the perfumes of Arabia will not sweeten
this little wine. Infirm of purpose. Thy lips rot off. It
would not even go with eating the bitter bread of
banishment. This wine was the most unkindest cut
of all. What fools these vintners be. Something is
rotten in the state of France.

ERNEST HEMINGWAY ON PORT

It was noon. So this is how it is, this is how it always
happens in the noon. Obscenity your noon. With my
last 50 francs I purchased some true and honest
port; I took a pull from the bottle. It was good. It
burned my mouth and felt good and warm going
down my esophagus and into my stomach. From
there it went to my kidneys and my bladder, and was
good. I remembered then when I last saw Scotty
Fitzgerald who was still a damn fine writer. It was in
Paris and we looked out the windows at the tree and
drank port in the noon. It was noon and had been
noon for some time.

IF FAMOUS AUTHORS & COMEDIANS WROTE ABOUT WINE

E.G. BULWER-LYTTON ON MERLOT

It was a dark and stormy wine that fell in torrents down my throat — except at occasional intervals, when it was checked by a violent piece of cork (for cork had been pushed into the bottle when it was incorrectly opened), rattling along my esophagus and fiercely agitating the inflamed tissue of my gullet that struggled against the tangy, fermented liquid.

HENNY YOUNGMAN ON MUSCAT

Take my wine ... please.

JOAN RIVERS ON CHABLIS

Can we talk? This wine seems like a man — shallow, shallow, shallow! But maybe that's because the glass wasn't filled. Speaking of glasses, I hate housework! You make the beds, you clean the wine glasses — and six months later you have to start all over again. I don't know what vintage this was but it was too young. The winemaker doesn't understand the concept of Roman numerals. She thought we just fought in world war eleven. Good wine is like sex. It's so long since I've had good wine I've forgotten who ties up who. And never floss with a stranger — especially after you drink this stuff. Oh, grow up!

DR. SEUSS ON CHAMPAGNE

I do not like it,
Cham-I-am.
I do not like
That pagne of cham

It sends bubbles up my nose
And makes me vomit on my toes
I do not like that
Cham-I-am

Would you like it here or there?

I would not like it here or there
I would not like it anywhere

Would you like it in a flute?

I would not like it in a flute
And even Horton wouldn't give a hoot

Would you like it if it's old?
Could you like it if its cold?

I would not like it if it's old
I could not like it if it's cold

I would not like it here or there
I would not like it anywhere
I do not like that pagne of Cham

IF FAMOUS AUTHORS & COMEDIANS WROTE ABOUT WINE

DEAR ABBEY ON GRENACHE

This wine made me see red. It doesn't just need to breathe — it needs to vent. And I'm pleased to pass along this important warning. However, I see no reason to panic. Only time will tell whether you and this wine have a future together — a lot of time. But stranger things have happened. I urge you and your friends to have a long talk about it. Be comforted in the knowledge that I probably reacted to this wine exactly as you will.

YOGI BERRA ON ZINFANDEL

It had deep depth.

CHARLES DICKENS ON SYRAH

It was the best of wines. It was the worst of wines. It had a hint of petulance. It had a hint of splendor. It had a bouquet deceptively grassy. It had a bouquet sharply rich in character. It had a texture soft and flabby. It had a texture tight and compressed. It had a silky harmony. It had an acidic harmony. It had an expressive sultry nuance. It had a hedonistic oily nuance. Drinking it was a far, far better thing than I have ever done before.

ERMA BOMBECK ON PINOT NOIR

Wine bottles stuck in the car cushions do not improve with time. Which explains why most women put off entertaining until the kids are grown. Every day of his or her life a child is plotting an event that will age you 20 years in 20 seconds. Now if they could only do that for wine. All of us have moments in our lives that test our courage. Taking a pinot noir and children into a house with white carpet is one of them. Anyway, the taste was OK and the price was alright. But how come anything you buy will go on sale next week?

WINE TASTING PHRASE CREATOR

Tired of pompous wine snobs and their pronouncements about agreeably earthy aftertaste or exquisitely sensuous bouquet? Fight back. Now you can speak their language and let them hear how they sound. Just pick three numbers between o and 15. Then combine the words that correspond to the numbers in the following three columns.

o	charmingly	o	nuanced	o	aftertaste
1	elegantly	1	citrusy	1	aroma
2	distinguished	2	fruity	2	bouquet
3	ponderous	3	robust	3	blend
4	well-balanced	4	herbaceous	4	body
5	austere	5	berry-like	5	varietal
6	subtly	6	creamy	6	vintage
7	full-bodied	7	gutsy	7	palate
8	mouth-filling	8	oaky	8	accent
9	rustic	9	musty	9	finish
10	agreeably	10	harmonious	10	character
11	ripe	11	precocious	11	flavor
12	exquisitely	12	sensuous	12	perfume
13	surprisingly	13	earthy	13	titration
14	powerful	14	intricate	14	nose
15	amusingly	15	bitter	15	taste

For example:

0-15-4	charmingly bitter body
7-3-10	full-bodied robust character
15-12-8	amusingly sensuous accent
4-11-9	well-balanced precocious finish
9-6-13	rustic creamy titration
5-0-11	austere nuanced flavor

You get the idea.

What if the results present two words which contradict each other? No problem. Just separate them with the word "yet." For example:

> *An austere yet nuanced flavor.*

> *A well-balanced yet precocious finish.*

You can sound even more pretentious by prefacing your phrase with "a bit of a." For example:

> *It has a bit of a rustic creamy titration.*

> *It has a bit of an austere yet nuanced flavor.*

Finally, for maximum pomposity, throw in a reference to PBS or foreign film. (I mean foreign cinema.) "This is the same vintage that the girlfriend drank in Il Postino. It has a bit of an austere yet nuanced flavor."

THE NEW 'NON-PRETENTIOUS' PRETENTIOUSNESS

In response to the traditional pompous wine-speak, a younger generation of critics, tasters and experts has created a new way of talking about wine. It abandons flowery phrases such as 'deceptively petulant angularity' and 'a hint of wistfully redolent corpulence.' Instead, it replaces them with much more direct similes, metaphors and analogies. Here are a few examples.

WINE: the Barry Bonds of wine – you just want to take a slug.

WINE: like a new Bonnie Rait CD – brash yet predictable and comfortable.

WINE: takes off like a civil servant at 5 o'clock on a Friday.

WINE: think of a sweaty T-shirt thrown by a rock star into a screaming crowd–pungent and in your face with a sense of anticipation.

WINE: like excuses you used to give for not doing your homework – unimaginative and hard to swallow.

WINE: a liquid version of a U.S. senator – well-aged, smooth and expensive.

On April 11, 2002, Internet news source Ananova reported that a group of 54 wine tasters in Bordeaux heaped praises on a red wine in an expensive bottle. There was just one problem. It was really a cheap white wine.

Psychologists conducting an experiment added tasteless food dye to a cheap white wine and placed the mixture in an expensive-looking bottle. None of the 'experts' detected the deception.

When tasted from the expensive bottle, the wine was called 'robust', 'fruity but charming' and 'marvelous'. When drunk from the proper bottle, it was called 'weak', 'thin' and 'too light'.

The tasters are still seeing red. But it has nothing to do with wine.

Chapter 7

TO BRIE OR NOT TO BRIE

———————•———————

AUTHOR ROBERT BYRNE ONCE SAID, "Partying is such sweet sorrow." He must have been talking about a wine and cheese party. (Or wine and nibbles as one pretentiously cute invitation put it.)

Whether you're attending or hosting one of these affairs, navigating the required rituals and repartee is no easy feat. Even if you're only making an appearance. Too often you'll find most of your time spent just trying to avoid making a major faux pas. Which wine goes with which food. Who's not talking to whom. Who is sleeping with whom. A bewildering array of social traps can leave even the most well-mannered person suffering from etiquette exhaustion.

In this chapter, you will learn to deftly traverse the minefield known as a cocktail party. A few bon mots here. A few knowing winks there. Suddenly the party is almost over and you haven't been gross, gauche or goofy. That wasn't so hard. Next time will be even easier — just don't show up.

And if you're really nervous, just recall the advice of Judith Martin, better known as 'Miss Manners'. She said, "If it's against state law, it's generally considered a breach of etiquette."

"Dinner at the Huntercombes' possessed only two dramatic features — the wine was a farce and the food a tragedy."

Anthony Powell

"A hard drinker, being at table, was offered grapes at dessert. 'Thank you,' said he, pushing the dish away from him, 'but I am not in the habit of taking my wine in pills'."

Anthelme Brillat-Savarin

"After all, what is your hosts' purpose in having a party? Surely not for you to enjoy yourself; if that were their sole purpose, they'd have simply sent champagne and women over to your place by taxi."

P. J. O'Rourke

"The best thing about a cocktail party is being asked to it."

Gerald Nachman

"It's all right, the white wine came up with the fish."

Herman J. Mankiewicz
after getting sick at a formal dinner

"Some people look good with white wine, some don't."

Donald Barthelme

"The telephone is a good way to talk to people with out having to offer them a drink."

Fran Lebowitz

"Called up the Bureau of Alcohol, Tobacco, and Firearms regional office and asked, 'What wine goes best with an M-16?' The guy who answered did his best to be helpful: 'That depends. What are you smoking?'"

Michael Maciolek

"If white wine goes with fish, do white grapes go with sushi?"

Stephen Wright

"When my mom got really mad, she would say, 'Your butt is my meat.' Not a particularly attractive phrase. And I always wondered, 'Now, what wine goes with that?'"

Jonathan Solomon

"Wine at business meals is a skirmish in a board-room war, played out on a linen table cloth. Your handling of wine, whether ordering it or just drinking it, matters more than you think to your colleagues."

Wall Street Journal, May 5, 2000

Nervous about ordering beverages at your next big client dinner? You should be! Forget the three-martini lunch. In today's global economy, wine is the drink of choice. And that gives you a lot of choices. Red. White. Light. Heavy. French. Californian. Aged. Young. And the list goes on — the wine list that is. Every choice you make will be scrutinized by your dinner companions. So don't let them tag you as someone who is 'a few bottles short of a case' or 'all goblet and no stem.' You know what I'm saying.

What if you don't know the difference between a gamay and a gamma ray? No problem. The Business Success Wine Seminar is the answer to your prayers. It will teach you everything you need to know to navigate the perilous seas of wine that must be crossed at any client dinner.

Discover the three T's of wine success: tasting, tipping and tippling. Find out how to fake French with the best of them. It's easy. It's fun. And it doesn't take long. In only a few short hours you can be transformed from slob to snob.

Through feedback, experimentation and validation, you will learn how to:

- Think outside the bottle
- Find a mission-critical wine
- Create a strategic alliance with a waiter
- Rightsize your palette
- Select impactful wines
- Increase face time with sommeliers
- Drill down a wine list
- Leverage your wine assets

And that's not all! If you enroll today, you can attend a special pre-seminar seminar at no extra cost! That's where you'll learn the answers to many of today's most perplexing wine-related business questions. These include:

-Where does champagne fit in a post-bubble economy?
- Does white wine go with red ink?
- Does tainted wine give pushback?
- What is the effect of wine on leadership vision?
- Should you pursue wine made from low-hanging fruit?

Don't waste time coping with small change. Sign up for the Business Success Wine Seminar right now and unleash the wine master within. Never be nervous about a client dinner again. Close your next big deal with a clink of crystal wine glasses. And, best of all, roll your eyes in disgust at faux pas committed by the unsophisticated.

Don't shake an old bottle of wine.
(Even if you tell everyone it's your 'medicine.)

Don't let your guests drive home inebriated.
(Do let them stay and puke all over your house.)

Don't fill a wineglass more than half full.
(Optimists will find this sufficient and pessimists will go nuts.)

Don't assume a cork in a bottle is a sign of quality.
(Especially if the cork is floating in the wine.)

Do pour wine with the label toward the guest so he or she can see what's in the bottle.
(Unless you're afraid of what's in it.)

Do store wines long term in a cool, dark place.
(But not your throat.)

Don't make sound effects when you drink wine.
(Especially gurgling.)

Do pick a gift wine that matches your host's tastes and interests.
(And carpet.)

It's not hazy.
It's clarity is charmingly opaque.

It's not bitter.
It's flavor has a sharp bite reminiscent of citric juices.

It's not moldy. *It's well-aged.*

It doesn't smell like rotten eggs.
It's got a pungent bouquet.

It's not full of sediment.
It's an earthy wine.

"Sorry, but you're going to have to remind me who gets the red wine and who gets the white?"

THE KID

A family that included a five-year-old child went to a fancy restaurant for dinner. After perusing the wine menu, the father ordered a bottle of 1965 Cabernet Sauvignon. When the wine steward returned, he performed the traditional ritual of uncorking the bottle and pouring a small amount for the father to taste. The five-year-old, watching all this, turned to the waiter and bellowed, "Daddy usually drinks a lot more than that."

A little girl watched as her parents dressed for a formal wine-tasting party. As her dad donned his tuxedo, she warned, "Daddy, you shouldn't wear that suit." "Why not?" he asked. The little girl replied, "It always gives you a headache the next morning."

"What's the right wine to go with severance pay?"

Chapter 8

TOASTED

CHEERS! SLAL! SLAINT! SALUTE! L'CHAIM! Every nationality has a word or phrase to say when you hoist a glass of wine. In fact, the tradition of toasting is as universal as wine drinking — and probably just as old. Whether it's health, wealth, birthdays or Earth Days, every wish and event provides an occasion for a toast.

And if you move in the worlds of diplomacy or international business, toasting can take on a symbolic importance far beyond the actual words you utter. Because when the words are forgotten, the gesture remains. Like the time during a ceremonial toast that a flu-stricken American president regurgitated on the feet of a Japanese prime minister. No one remembers what was said. But that toast has become immortalized.

In this chapter, you will find some ideas for making an amusing toast — without puking on the toastee. A whole range of techniques is covered, from definitions to rhymes to curses.

So when it's time for you to toast.
You'll never be at a loss.
And you'll be able to get a smile.
Without doing a dinner toss.

As a peeping Tom once said while toasting his prey, "Here's looking at you kid."

In the words of Groucho Marx:
"I drink to your charm, your beauty and your brains
—which gives you a rough idea of how hard up I am
for a drink."

In the words of Lem Motlow:
"To temperance . . . in moderation."

In the words of Mark Twain:
"Let us toast the fools; but for them the rest of us
could not succeed."

In the words of Lou Crane:
"Here's a toast — To those who challenge us to mind
games, but forget to bring their equipment!"

In the words of P.J. O'Rourke:
"It is better to spend money like there's no tomorrow then to spend tonight like there's no money."

In the words of Jonathan Swift:
"May you live all the days of your life."

In the words of Ambrose Bierce:
"Marriage: A community consisting of a master,
a mistress, and two slaves — making in all, two."

MAY

May your dreams come true if you ever wake up.

May you have more blessings than sneezes.

May your life be fine and may you never pay one.

May the IRS never audit your thoughts.

May all your tomorrows come in the future.

May your men be like grapes on the vine — well rounded and well hung.

May what goes down not come back up again.

"What do you have in investment-grade reds?"

TO

To nepotism —
it's the only thing holding our family together.

To success —
a mythological state of mind in which you're happy.

To friendship —
the only ship that sinks without taking on water.

To age —
it comes before beauty — especially in your case.

To wealth and health —
you need one to pay for the other.

To good friends —
if you want one, get a dog.

To peace of mind —
I'd like to give you a piece of mine.

To foolishness —
it's more fun than Elliot Ness.

To love —
an imagined feeling shared by two people who have
not yet killed each other.

To the future —
a time in which you haven't screwed up yet.

To truth —
the last refuge of a person with imagination.

To influence —
you either have it or you're under it.

To laughter —
a wonderful sound that people make when they
think of you.

To travel and adventure —
the journey of a thousand miles begins with the first
drink.

To eternity —
may it last forever!

RHYMING TOASTS

Here's to you
Get well quick
In fact I hope
You're not even sick

•

May your heart be filled with joy
Your Chinese food flavored with soy
But your vay never joined with an oy

•

I'm not sure
Exactly what this means
But may your crystal ball
Be filled with jellybeans

•

Despite our differences
I'm sure you'll agree
The best words you can hear
Are the drinks are on me

•

I'll drink to this
I'll drink to that
I'll drink to anything
Till I'm on the floor flat

•

God in His goodness sent the grapes
To cheer both great and small
Little fools will drink too much
And great fools not at all

Want an easy way to give a memorable toast and get a laugh? Just put a curse on the person you're toasting and conclude with the words 'Heaven forbid.' For example, "May you grow beets in your belly and pee borsht — heaven forbid." "May the devil cut the head off you and make a day's work of your neck — heaven forbid." You get the idea.

Good material for this type of toast comes from the traditional curses common to various ethnic groups. Here are a few to get you started.

May you be afflicted with the itch and have no nails to scratch with!

Irish curse

•

May the fleas of a thousand camels lodge in your armpit.

Arab curse

•

May you win a lottery, and spend it all on doctors.

Jewish curse

•

May your life be filled with lawyers!

Mexican curse

Of course, you're not limited to using ancient ethnic curses. The technique applies to any curse. And it works particularly well if you write your own contemporary curses. For example: May you be trapped in a house where the TV can only play what's in the VCR and the only videos available are Sylvester Stallone's comedies – heaven forbid! Here are a few more ideas.

May your teenager win a scholarship to trumpet school.

•

May a telemarketer find your unlisted phone number on a bathroom wall.

•

May the outcome of your election depend on votes from Florida.

•

May the liposuction from your thighs go to your cheeks.

•

May your coupons expire the day before you use them.

•

May a disease be named after you.

•

May CourtTV broadcast your trial.

•

May your daughter be a guest on the Jerry Springer Show.

Chapter 9

CHAMPAGNE WISHES AND CAVIAR SCREAMS

CHAMPAGNE WISHES AND CAVIAR SCREAMS

———————•———————

A 17TH CENTURY MONK NAMED Dom Pérignon is often credited with adding the bubbles to champagne. Upon tasting his invention, he exclaimed, "I'm drinking stars." Today, after drinking his discovery, many of us are seeing stars. But there's no doubt that there's something special about champagne.

Traditionally called the wine of kings, champagne is treated differently than other types of wine.

A few examples. No one ever launches a ship by breaking a bottle of beaujolais over the bow. No one ever drinks zinfandel out of a golden slipper. And no one ever opens a bottle of merlot by cracking its neck with a sword.

This last custom—called 'beheading'—dates from the time of Napoleon. It refers to the way his officers opened champagne bottles with their sabres. And it gives a whole new meaning to the psychobabble phrase 'opening up'.

In this chapter, you will find some amusing lines and lore about champagne. Everything from court testimony to scientific principles. As an old ecology philosopher once said, "conserve water, drink champagne."

OBSERVATIONS ABOUT CHAMPAGNE

"Champagne is the answer. I don't remember the question."

Unknown

"The quality of a champagne is judged by the amount of noise the cork makes when it is popped."

Unknown

"Champagne is the wine a young man drinks on the evening of his first mistake."

Unknown

"I like champagne because it always tastes as though my foot's asleep."

Art Buchwald

"You can have too much champagne to drink but you can never have enough."

Elmer Rice

"If you're given champagne at lunch, there's a catch somewhere."

Lord Lyons

"In victory, you deserve champagne; in defeat, you need it."

Napoleon

OBSERVATIONS ABOUT CHAMPAGNE

"I drink champagne when I'm happy and when I'm sad. Sometimes I drink it when I'm alone. When I have company, I consider it obligatory. Otherwise I never touch it— unless I'm thirsty."

Elizabeth Bollinger

"The House of Lords is like a glass of champagne that has stood for five days."

Clement Attlee

"You've forgotten those June nights at the Riviera...the night I drank champagne from your slipper—two quarts. It would have been more but you were wearing inner soles."

Groucho Marx

"Here's to champagne, the drink divine that makes us forget our troubles. It's made of a dollar's worth of wine and three dollar's worth of bubbles."

Anonymous

"A bottle of Mouton Lafitte Rothschild sold at auction for $80,000. It is one of the oldest unopened bottles of champagne in existence. It was discovered in storage in the Chicago Cubs locker room."

Argus Hamilton

Renowned wit Oscar Wilde expressed his love of the bubbly on April 4, 1895 in an exchange in court during his prosecution of the Marquess of Queensberry for criminal libel. (Regina [Wilde] v. Queensberry.)

Mr. Edward Carson, QC:
Do you drink champagne yourself?

Mr. Oscar Wilde:
Yes; iced champagne is a favourite drink of mine—strongly against my doctor's orders.

Mr. Edward Carson, QC:
Never mind your doctor's orders, sir!

Mr. Oscar Wilde:
I never do.

If the quantity and temperature of a gas remain constant, its volume will vary inversely with pressure.

That's known as Boyle's law. (It's named after its discoverer, Sir Robert Boyle.) You might have learned it in a high school chemistry class. But forget about test-tubes. Boyle's law has major implications for champagne.

According to the March 1973 issue of Chem 13 News, a group of politicians went under a river during construction of a tunnel in order to celebrate the meeting of the two shafts. Naturally, they drank champagne. But they were disappointed. The carbon-dioxide bubbles remained in solution because the champagne was under depth pressure. When the politicians returned to the surface, they were in for a surprise. The champagne popped in their stomachs, distended their vests and almost came out their ears. One of them had to go back in the tunnel to undergo champagne recompression.

Conclusion:
1. Boyle's law applies to champagne.
2. Politicians are always full of hot air.

FIZZ WIZ

On January 18, 2002, the Hindustan Times reported that the bubbles in champagne get you drunk more quickly. Research conducted by Fran Ridout at the University of Surrey showed that alcohol levels rose faster in volunteers drinking fizzy champagne compared with those drinking flat champagne.

It gives a whole new meaning to the phrase 'bubble brain'.

THE GIFT

On the last day of kindergarten, all the children brought presents for their teacher. The florist's son handed the teacher a gift. She shook it, held it up and said, "I bet I know what it is— it's some flowers!" "That's right!" shouted the little boy. Then the candy store owner's daughter handed the teacher a gift. She held it up, shook it and said. "I bet I know what it is - it's a box of candy!" "That's right!" shouted the little girl. The next gift was from the wine store owner's son. The teacher held it up and saw that it was leaking. She touched a drop with her finger and tasted it. "Is it wine?" she asked. "No," said the little boy. The teacher touched another drop to her tongue. "Is it champagne?" she asked. "No," he answered. Finally, the teacher said, "I give up. What is it?" The little boy replied, "A puppy!"

You are more likely to be killed by a champagne cork than by a poisonous spider.

A raisin dropped into a glass of champagne will repeatedly bounce up and down between the top and the bottom of the glass.

Marilyn Monroe is said to have taken a bath in 350 bottles of champagne.

The pressure in a bottle of Champagne is 90 pounds per square inch, about three times that in an auto tire.

The hobby of collecting champagne bottle tops is called plaquemusephilia.

The speed of a popped champagne cork has been estimated at anywhere from 35 to 100 miles per hour when it leaves the bottle.

The Concorde flies 10 miles in the time it takes to fill a champagne glass.

The champagne used for James Bond films was actually ginger ale.

Chapter 10

DAYS OF WINE & ROSÉS

OSCAR WILDE ONCE SAID, "Experience is simply the name we give our mistakes." Keep that in mind the next time you hear people talk about their vast experience with wine. The most experienced may be the most mistaken.

Of course, the ability to detect a mistake depends on who committed it. As architect Frank Lloyd Wright observed, "A doctor can bury his mistakes but an architect can only advise his client to plant vines." Unfortunately for wine lovers, a vintner who makes a mistake has already planted vines.

Wine-related mistakes are certainly not limited to vintners. They're also made by merchants, consumers, tasters, waiters and all the other characters inhabiting the world of wine. In this chapter, we'll examine some of the more amusing consequences resulting from their mistakes.

Think about them. Learn from them. And you'll be better able to follow the advice of Tallulah Bankhead who said, "If I had to live my life again, I'd make the same mistakes, only sooner."

According to legend, a Persian who loved grapes stored several bunches in a large jar labeled 'poison.' Some time later, a despondent member of his harem drank from the jar in an attempt to take her life. But by then the poison was so delicious that she revived. She immediately took a cup to the king. After drinking it, he restored the woman to favor and proclaimed that thereafter grapes should be allowed to ferment. And that is said to be the origin of wine.

What can we learn from this story?

1. *The way to a man's heart is through his stomach.*

2. *Wine is poison for the young and medicine for the old.*

3. *It is cheap to eat grapes in the other man's vineyard.*

4. *Appearances are deceiving.*

5. *Don't judge a book by its cover.*

6. *If you're a member of a harem who wants to kill herself, buy your own poison.*

CLUES YOU'RE BUYING WINE AT THE WRONG STORE

1. Proprietor gives samples in a Big Gulp cup.

2. You get a free bottle with a fill-up.

3. At checkout counter your bottle is placed in a barf bag.

4. Window display features a man hiccupping.

5. Accepts coupons from competitors – Home Depot and Ace Hardware.

6. Proprietor says dust on bottles shows they're well-aged.

7. Sales clerk looks like he's drunk all the inventory.

MORE LAWS OF WINE

"Avoid any wine with a childproof cap."

Richard Smith

"Never drink from your finger bowl — it contains only water."

Addison Mizner

"If you drink, don't drive. Don't even putt."

Dean Martin

"The only thing that should come between people and wine is the cork."

Andrea Immer

"Great people talk about ideas, average people talk about things, and small people talk about wine."

Fran Lebowitz

"It is useless to hold a person to anything he says while he's in love, drunk, or running for office."

Shirley MacLaine

"There are three principal ways to lose money: wine, women, and engineers. While the first two are more pleasant, the third is by far the more certain."

Baron Rothschild

"You can tell German wine from vinegar by the label."

Mark Twain

"It's a cheap party if you have to drink beer in wine glasses!"

Alfred Molina

"Burgundy makes you think of silly things; Bordeaux makes you talk about them, and Champagne makes you do them."

Anthelme Brillat-Savarin

"The best wine is the oldest, the best water the newest."

William Blake

"Compromises are for relationships, not wine."

Sir Robert Scott Caywood

A gentleman invited some friends over for a dinner party. Late in the evening he decided to open a very old bottle of wine from the back of his wine cellar. When he popped the cork, out came a Genie rather than wine. "For releasing me from that bottle, I will give you a choice of two gifts. You can either choose great wisdom or a handful of gold coins," the Genie offered.

The gentleman thought for a moment. Not wanting to appear greedy he said, "I choose wisdom over wealth." The Genie touched him on the forehead, which produced a blinding light, and then disappeared in a puff of smoke.

The friends all stared at their friend. After a period of silence, one inquired respectfully, "Now that you have great wisdom, what can you share with the rest of us?" The gentleman looked at his friends and replied thoughtfully, "I should have taken the money."

A clergyman is driving and gets stopped for speeding. The policeman smells alcohol on the his breath and then sees a half-empty wine bottle clasped between his legs. He says, "Excuse me, but have you been drinking?" "No, Oshifer. It's jusht water," answers the clergyman. The policeman grabs the bottle, takes off the lid and gives it a sniff. He says, "Uh-uh, this is most definitely wine." The clergyman takes the bottle and takes a swig. "Good Lord!" he says, "He's done it again!"

Two guys were on a ship in the middle of the ocean when it was hit by a big storm. As the ship sank, the two guys escaped in a small lifeboat with provisions for a few days.

After almost a week, they thought they were goners. Just then, one of the guys spotted a bottle floating next to the lifeboat. He pulled it from the ocean and, after giving it a quick rub, a genie popped out. "I am a genie, and I will grant you one wish," said the genie.

The guy who found the bottle replied, "I wish I had something to drink!" "Granted." The genie disappeared and the ocean turned into wine. "Great move Einstein!" said the other guy. "Now we have to spit in the boat."

Get a Whiff of This

On March 15, 2002, web news service Ananova reported that wine lovers will be able to virtually smell their favorite vineyards while surfing the Internet. A device which attaches to a PC will allow users to sniff the "vine shoots or the smell of a musty cellar" in Burgundy. Developed by France Telecom and ACII, the devise can give the synchronized diffusion of 12 scents.

It could give a whole new meaning to scratch and sniff.

Guys Definitely Make Passes at Girls With Smart Glasses

On April 5, 2002, it was reported that scientists at Mitsubishi Electric Research Laboratories in Cambridge, Massachusetts invented a wineglass that automatically alerts waiters when a refill is needed. The key is a microchip built into the base of the glass. When the wine in the glass falls below a certain level, the chip sends a signal that's relayed to a waiter or bartender. Each chip stores a unique digital code for a specific wine glass.

Now if they could just create a microchip that alerts you when you've had enough.

Source: www.bbr.com

Chapter 11

───────────●───────────

I'LL DRINK TO THAT

———————————•———————————

A NEWSPAPER TV LISTING allegedly described 'The Wizard of Oz' as follows: "Transported to a surreal landscape, a young girl kills the first woman she meets and then teams up with three complete strangers to kill again." The story may be apocryphal, but there's no doubt that newspapers are increasingly filled with strange items. As columnist Art Buchwald has observed, "You can't make up anything anymore. The world itself is a satire. All you're doing is recording it." And that's especially true in the world of wine.

In this chapter, you will find several accounts of unusual wine-related events, occurrences, discoveries and laws. They range from criminal activity to scientific research. And they're all of the hard-to-believe-but-true variety. Embrace them. Celebrate them. Drink to them.

We live in an amazing world that produces amazing news. And as comedian Jerry Seinfeld has observed, "It's amazing that the amount of news that happens in the world every day always just exactly fits the newspaper."

"I feel sorry for people who don't drink. When they wake up in the morning, that's as good as they're going to feel all day."

Frank Sinatra

"When I read about the evils of drinking, I gave up reading."

Henny Youngman

"Not all men who drink are poets. Some of us drink because we aren't poets."

Unknown

"I drink to make other people interesting."

George Jean Nathan

"I drink to forget I drink."

Joe E. Lewis

"I don't drink because I have problems or I want to escape. I just love drinking and being drunk."

Richard Harris

"I don't drink; I don't like it — it makes me feel good."

Oscar Levant

"The only time I ever said no to a drink was when I misunderstood the question."

Will Sinclair

"My grandmother is over eighty and still doesn't need glasses. Drinks right out of the bottle."

Henny Youngman

"If you resolve to give up smoking, drinking and loving, you don't actually live longer; it just seems longer."

Clement Freud

"If your doctor warns that you have to watch your drinking, find a bar with a mirror."

John Mooney

"I've got a drinking problem—two hands and only one mouth."

Unknown

"I've stopped drinking, but only while I'm asleep."

George Best

"I haven't touched a drop of alcohol since the invention of the funnel."

Malachy McCourt

"I don't drink anymore – just the same amount."

Joe. E. Lewis

"I've formed a new group called Alcoholics Unanimous. If you don't feel like a drink, you ring another member and he comes over to persuade you."

Richard Harris

OBSERVATIONS ON DRINKING

"I don't have a drink problem except when I can't get one."

Tom Waits

"If I give up drinking, smoking, and fatty foods, I can add ten years to my life. Trouble is, I'll add it to the wrong end."

P.J. O'Rourke

"I am not a heavy drinker. I can sometimes go for hours without touching a drop."

Noel Coward

"I envy people who drink. At least they have some thing to blame everything on."

Oscar Levant

"If you drink like a fish, don't drive. Swim."

Joe E. Lewis

"I only drink wine when I am alone or with someone."

Unknown

It's illegal to feed a moose any alcoholic beverage in Fairbanks, Alaska.
(So if you're on a date, take the moose to Canada.)

In Columbia, Missouri, you can't drink in a bar between 2:00 and 6:00 AM.
(But you can puke your brains out for four hours and then start drinking again.)

In Rehoboth Beach, Delaware, alcohol may not be served in nightclubs if dancing is occurring on the premises at the same time.
(It's unclear if hopping from one foot to the other while waiting to use the restroom constitutes dancing.)

In Arvada, Colorado, establishments that sell alcohol must have enough lighting for customers to read the label text.
(Because it's hard enough to read the label when you're seeing double.)

Ohio state law prohibits getting a fish drunk.
(But it's OK if you want to drink like one.)

In California, no alcoholic beverages can be displayed within five feet of a cash register at any store that sells both alcohol and motor fuel.
(Yes, it's so easy to confuse the two—I'll take three gallons of the unleaded premium with the rustic, berry-like after-taste.)

It's been said that truth is stranger than fiction. Whoever said it must have read some of the following accounts of wine in the news.

WAS IT A PINK ELEPHANT?

On July 1998, the Russian news agency ITAR-Tass reported that an elephant in the Moscow zoo celebrated its first birthday by guzzling a 10-liter magnum of champagne. The champagne, a birthday gift from the elephant's zookeepers, was offered in a bucket. After downing the bubbly, the elephant consumed a gargantuan fruitcake as a chaser.

Well, you'd have to be drunk to eat a whole fruitcake.

WOMAN DOES GET A KICK FROM CHAMPAGNE

According to Russian news service Pravda, a woman was almost killed when a bottle of champagne exploded in her pocket. Fortunately onlookers took her to a local clinic where she received treatment in time to save her life. The woman said she would sue the champagne maker.

Forget about malatov cocktails. The heavy artillery is now champagne bombs.

RADIOACTIVE WINE

According to News of the Weird, in December 1996, scientists at the Japan Atomic Power Co. announced stunning test results with implications for winos around the world. Their experiments showed that the taste of cheap wine could be improved by bombarding it with deadly doses of gamma rays.

Who volunteered to taste it?

BEER VS. WINE

According to News of the Weird, a study of 12,000 people by University of North Carolina researchers, revealed that people who drink lots of beer have large bellies but most people who drink lots of wine don't.

Duh!

LITTLE ROSE RIDING HOOD

On April 23, 1990, the New York Times reported that 400 copies of 'Little Red Riding Hood' were locked in a public school district storage room in Empire, California. Why? The fairy tale mentions that the little girl brought her grandmother a bottle of wine.

Grandma, what big bloodshot eyes you have.

In February 2002, the Associated Press reported the firing of five bankers employed by Barclay's Capital. Their offense? The prior summer they, and a sixth banker, celebrated a business deal by going out to dinner.

The total bill was $62,679 — called the most expensive meal per capita ever by Guinness World Records. It included a $16,500 bottle of 1945 Chateau Petrus Bordeaux; a $13,400 bottle of the 1946 vintage; and a $17,500 bottle from 1947. The dessert wine cost $13,100.

It would have cost even more if they'd left a tip.

According to the BBC News, in November 2001 thieves hijacked a wine truck in London and stole 18,500 bottles of wine. In a separate incident, thieves stole three tons of mozzarella cheese from a truck in Shropshire. Police, looking for leads, have appealed to anyone being offered large quantities of mozzarella cheese.

They'd also like to speak with anyone who was invited to a three-month wine and cheese party.

"Typical trust-fund red from a vanity vintner."

Chapter 12

TO YOUR HEALTH

———————————•———————————

MARK TWAIN ONCE SAID, "The only way to keep your health is to eat what you don't want, drink what you don't like, and do what you'd rather not." That might have been true in Twain's time, but it's not anymore. Recent scientific research suggests that people who drink moderate amounts of wine each day are healthier and live longer than teetotalers.

Of course, the definition of 'moderate' is open to interpretation. It's probably somewhat less than the amount consumed by Frances Rabelais. He's the classical French writer who said, "I drink no more than a sponge."

And it's definitely less than the consumption of legendary film-maker Orson Welles. He once said, "My doctor told me to stop having intimate dinners for four. Unless there are three other people."

In this chapter, we will examine the humorous aspects of wine and health — both mental and physical. Because wine drinking has been credited with everything from improving mood to extending longevity. And as George Burns observed, "If you live to be one hundred, you've got it made. Very few people die past that age."

"Health is what my friends are always drinking to before they fall down."

Phyllis Diller

"I'm like old wine. They don't bring me out very often, but I'm well preserved."

Rose Kennedy on her 100th birthday

"I have made an important discovery...that alcohol, taken in sufficient quantities, produces all the effects of intoxication."

Oscar Wilde

"It seems that researchers at Colorado University say wine may help people lose weight. It's not the wine directly that causes the weight loss, it's all the walking around you do trying to find your car."

Jay Leno

"What is man, when you come to think upon him, but a minutely set, ingenious machine for turning, with infinite artfulness, the red wine of Shiraz into urine?"

Isak Dinesen

"Never accept a drink from a urologist."

Erma Bombeck

"All wines have nutritional value. If you don't buy, we don't eat."

Sign in a restaurant

"A mind of the calibre of mine cannot derive its nutriment from cows."

George Bernard Shaw

"A well-balanced person has a drink in each hand."

Billy Connolly

"The secret to a long life is to stay busy, get plenty of exercise and don't drink too much. Then again, don't drink too little."

Hermann Smith-Johannson,
103-year-old cross-country skier

"A psychologist once said that we know little about the conscience—except that it is soluble in alcohol."

Thomas Blackburn

"Alcohol is necessary for a man so that he can have a good opinion of himself, undisturbed by the facts."

Finley Peter Dunne

1. The Japanese eat very little fat and suffer fewer heart attacks than the British or Americans.

2. The French eat a lot of fat and also suffer fewer heart attacks than the British or Americans.

3. The Japanese drink very little red wine and suffer fewer heart attacks than the British or Americans.

4. The Italians drink excessive amounts of red wine and also suffer fewer heart attacks than the British or Americans.

Conclusion: Eat and drink what you like. It's speaking English that kills you.

WHY WINE DRINKERS ARE HEALTHIER
THAN BEER DRINKERS

1. No wine gut.

2. Good wine costs too much to have guzzling contests.

3. Wine doesn't come in six packs.

4. No wine goes with peanuts.

5. Wine samples don't come in mugs.

6. Wine drinkers don't sit around all day saying 'Whazzup.'

A BAD DAY

A guy is sitting at a bar staring at his glass of wine.
He stays like that for an hour. Then a truck driver
walks up next to him, takes the wine and drinks it all
down. The guy starts crying. The truck driver says,
"I was only joking. I'll buy you another glass of wine.
I can't stand to see a man cry."

The guy stops crying and says, "It's just that this has
been the worst day of my life. First, I'm late to my
office. So my boss fires me. When I leave the build-
ing to go to my car, I find out it was stolen. The
police say they can't do anything. So I take a cab
home. And I leave my wallet and credit cards in the
cab. But I don't realize it till the cab is gone. And
when I go in my house, I find my wife in bed with the
gardener.

So I leave home and come to this bar and think
about killing myself." The truck driver says," Yeah,
that's a bad day." And the guy says, "Then you
showed up and drank my poison."

A man walked into a bar and ordered a glass of wine. He took a sip then tossed the remainder into the bartender's face. Before the bartender could recover, the man began weeping. "I'm sorry," he said. "I'm really sorry. I keep doing that to bartenders. It's a compulsion and I can't tell you how embarrassing it is." The bartender was sympathetic.

After chatting awhile, he suggested that the man see an analyst about his problem. "I have the name of a psychoanalyst," said the bartender. "My friends have been treated by him and they say he's very good."

Six months later, the man was back. "Did you go to the analyst?" asked the bartender as he served the man a glass of wine. "Yes," said the man. "I've been seeing him twice a week." He took a sip of the wine then he threw the remainder into the bartender's face. As the bartender wiped his face with a towel, he said, "The analyst doesn't seem to be doing you any good." "No," said the man, "he's done me alot of good." The puzzled bartender said, "But you threw the wine in my face again!" "Yes," said the man, "but it doesn't embarrass me anymore."

A man visits his doctor and tells him that he hasn't been feeling well. The doctor examines him, leaves the room and comes back with three different bottles of pills. The doctor says, "Take the green pill with a glass of wine when you get up. Take the blue pill with a glass of wine after lunch. Then, just before going to bed, take the red pill with another glass of wine." Surprised to have to take so much medicine, the man stammers, "Doc, what's wrong with me?" And the doctor says, "You're not drinking enough wine."

A wine aficionado felt sick and decided to go see the doctor. "I feel tired all the time, my head hurts, and I'm not sleeping. What is it, Doc?" After examining him, the doctor says, "Well, I can't find the exact problem, but I think it has to do with wine consumption." The fellow replies, "No problem, I'll just come back when you're sober!"

"Not much—just flushing out my arteries."

Quaffing and Laughing

Alcohol drinkers laugh more than non-alcohol drinkers, according to a study conducted by psychologists at the University of Hull in England. This increased laughter resulted not only from the affects of alcohol but from the anticipation of drinking alcohol. The study concluded that consuming alcohol leads to heightened anticipation and enjoyment.

Duh!

Hung Out But Not Over

On October 23, 2001, it was reported that University of British Columbia Professor Hennie van Vuuren created a wine that won't cause a hangover. It's made with genetically modified yeast patented by the professor. He has already produced several barrels of wine using his yeast.

It's already giving manufacturers of aspirin and ice-packs a big headache.

Source: www.bbr.com

A New Addiction?

On June 7, 2001, ABCNews.com reported that wine makers in Southern France planned to sell powdered wine to pharmaceutical companies. Why? So it could be made into pills. Why? So people could enjoy the health benefits of wine without getting a hangover.

Like we're not popping enough pills already.

The IQs Have It

In December 2000, the BBC News reported that Japanese researchers found that moderate drinking could boost brain power. Researchers at the National Institute for Longevity Sciences near Tokyo tested the IQs of 2,000 people. Men who drank a moderate daily amount of wine or sake had an IQ 3.3 points higher than teetotalers. Women drinkers tested 2.5 IQ points higher.

People who drank more than a moderate amount may also have higher IQs, but they passed out before the test was given.

Nothing to Sneeze At

On May 8, 2002, Reuters Health reported a study from Spain that found drinking wine can help prevent catching a cold. Conducted by Dr. Bahi Takkouche at University of Santiago de Compostela in Spain and Dr. Miguel A. Hernan at Harvard School of Public Health in Boston, the research showed that people who drank more than 14 glasses of wine per week had 40% fewer colds than teetotalers. Even people who drank only one glass of wine a day had fewer colds. And red wine worked better than white wine.

Or maybe people who drank more than 14 glasses of wine per week just didn't know they had a cold.

Chapter 13

DRIBBLINGS

COMEDIAN STEVEN WRIGHT once said, "you can't have everything. Where would you put it?" To prove him wrong I've tried to give you everything about wine humor in this book. Where did I put it? Simple. Anything that didn't fit elsewhere is in this chapter. It's where you'll find a wide variety of wine-related comic musings free from the tyranny of common theme. OK, so it's the miscellaneous chapter. As Joel Rosenberg observed, "Miscellaneous is always the largest category."

But please don't consider this a chapter of leftovers in the negative sense of the term. It's not the type of leftovers writer Calvin Trillan has referred to. Especially when he wrote, "The most remarkable thing about my mother is that for thirty years she served the family nothing but leftovers. The original meal has never been found." The leftovers in this chapter just didn't fit anywhere else.

In this chapter, you will find everything from philosophy and mythology to investment advice. It's an assortment of amusement. A Whitman's Sampler of wine humor. But don't despair about the lack of organization. The chapter is modeled on the words of Robert Frost, who said, "I'm not confused. I'm just well mixed."

Have you ever wanted to sound sophisticated while referring to a group of wine-related people? It's difficult. Because calling them a "group" or a "bunch" lacks sparkle and pizzazz. It's easier to sound chic talking about a bunch of animals. Then you can say a bevy of quail or a gaggle of geese. So why not create some specialized terms that apply to wine people? Here are some suggestions.

A snob of sommeliers.

A barrel of wine makers

A guzzle of wine tasters.

A pretense of wine critics.

A tipple of wine drinkers.

A killjoy of wine regulators.

A bubble of champagne vendors.

INVESTMENT ADVICE

If you bought $1,000 worth of Worldcom stock on July 2, 2001, one year later it would be worth $6.75.

If you bought $1,000 worth of wine, (at an average of $10 a bottle) one year ago, drank all the wine, and traded in the bottles for the 15 cent deposit in Maine, you would have $15.00.

Conclusion: Drink a lot of wine and recycle.

The famous guru was dying. His followers gathered around his bed, trying to make him comfortable. They gave him some warm milk to drink, but he refused it. Then his assistant took the glass back to the kitchen. Remembering a bottle of wine received as a gift, he opened it and poured a generous amount into the warm milk. Back at the guru's bed, the assistant held the glass to the guru's lips. The guru drank a little, then a little more, then before they knew it, he had drunk the whole glass down to the last drop. "Master. Master," the followers cried. "Give us some words of wisdom before you die!" The guru raised himself up in bed, pointed out the window, and said, "Don't sell that cow!"

"I have it on the highest medical authority that I will still be alive at the turn of the century!" She is thrilled. "You know what this means?" she asks. "Of course I know what it means. It means we do not have to drink up all our 1985 and 1986 Chateau Latour at supper tonight for fear I might die with several outrageously priced wines undrunk. For the first time in years, we can go to bed sober."

From The New York Times, May 12, 1990

A typical wine writer was once described as someone with a typewriter who was looking for his name
in print, a free lunch and a way to write off his wine
cellar. It's a dated view. Wine writers now use com-
puters.

Frank Prial,
The NY Times,
January 21, 1998

Filmmaker/winemaker Francis Ford Coppola says
the two professions are almost the same and that
each depends on source material and takes a lot of
time to perfect. The big difference: Today's wine-
makers still worry about quality.

Arizona Republic,
January 22, 1998

The butler was caught taking a swig from the red
wine that was to be served with dinner. He denied
having any compulsion to drink. "I had opened the
bottle to allow it to breathe," he explained.
"But it wasn't doing very well, so I tried to give it
some artificial respiration."

K. L. Jones
Saturday Evening Post,
Nov. 2000, Small Masterpieces

The best use of bad wine is to drive away poor relations.

French Proverb

The church is near, but the road is icy. The bar is far away, but I will walk carefully.

Russian Proverb

Man does not suffer from too much to drink, but from the hangover.

Russian Proverb

There are more old drunkards than old doctors.

French Proverb

One drink is just right; two is too many; three are too few.

Spanish Proverb

THE THIRSTY MAN

A man goes into a wine bar and seats himself on a stool. The bartender looks at him and says, "What'll it be, buddy?" The man says, "Give me seven glasses of the house white." The bartender does this and watches the man slug one down, then the next, then the next, and so on until all seven are gone almost as quickly as they were served. Staring in disbelief, the bartender asks why he's doing all this drinking. "You'd drink them this fast too if you had what I have." The bartender hastily asks, "What do you have pal?" The man quickly replies, "I have a dollar."

THE WARNING

A man was drinking at a bar when the bartender came over to tell him he had a telephone call. The man had just bought a glass of wine and he didn't want anyone to drink it. So he wrote a little sign and left it by his glass. It said: "I spit in my wine." When the man returned to his bar-stool there was another note beside his glass: "I spit in your wine too!"

1. A morbid, irrational fear of or aversion to wine is called...
    a. Winephobia
    b. Oenophobia
    c. Wineophobia

2. The American corkscrew was invented in...
    a. 1860
    b. 1840
    c. a hurry

3. A popular myth is that champagne glasses
    were molded from the breasts of...
    a. Helen of Troy
    b. Marie Antoinette
    c. Louis VIII

4. In the Middle Ages, wine was used as...
    a. Currency
    b. Paint
    c. Make-up

5. Robert Louis Stevenson referred to wine as...
    a. Umm, umm good
    b. Bottled rhapsody
    c. Bottled poetry

6. The indentation at the bottom of some
    wine bottles is called a...
    a. Punt
    b. Dent
    c. Mistake

7. Headaches from drinking red wine
   are caused by...
   > a. Histamines in the wine
   > b. Paying the bill
   > c. Passing out and hitting your head

8. The marks made by wine as it runs
   down a glass are called...
   > a. Legs
   > b. Arms
   > c. Marks

9. Phylloxera is...
   > a. A tiny aphid-like insect
   > b. A wine-growing region in France
   > c. A chemical in grapes

10. Approximately how many calories are
    in a glass of dry, white wine?
    > a. 210
    > b. 340
    > c. depends on the size of the glass

11. Wine is swirled in a glass to...
    > a. Activate the aromas
    > b. Redistribute the sediment
    > c. Make you look cool

12. The air space between the surface of the wine and the cork in a sealed bottle is called...
    a. Ullage
    b. Air space
    c. A rip-off

13. Horizontal tasting is...
    a. Tasting the same wine from different vintage years
    b. Tasting different wines with something in common from the same year
    c. Tasting any wine after you've fallen over

14. Most incidents of spoiled wine are due to...
    a. Bacteria turning alcohol to vinegar
    b. Oxidation of the fruit
    c. Obnoxious companions

ANSWERS

1.	b	8.	a
2.	a	9.	a
3.	b	10.	c
4.	a	11.	a
5.	c	12.	a
6.	a	13.	b
7.	a	14.	b

Aftertaste

ACKNOWLEDGMENTS

Many people helped bring this book into existence. First and foremost was Annette Leibl who had the idea and nagged me into doing it. Christine Griger provided her usual impeccable editing.

Rachael Brune's design and John Claude Hundt's illustrations gave the book its classy look. And Bob Reed provided all-around publishing expertise and hand-holding throughout the entire process.

Also providing encouragement or critiques were Pat O'Brien and Lanny Stover; Bob Dufau, Marnie Dufau and Heather Dufau; Linda Bindler; Dennis Leibl; Allison Spiller; Lu Haussler; and Sam R. Kushner. I've also got to thank Bob Schwartz for the wine jokes he found on the web. I salute you all.

SOURCES

Cartoons: Licensed from Cartoonbank.com
Quotations and news items: The sources for these items
are identified as they appear in the book.
Jokes and anecdotes: Many were compiled from the
Internet. Like folklore, they're familiar to all of us but
their authors are unknown.The sources for other comic
material used in the book are as follows.

CHAPTER 1

Everything I Need to Know I Learned From Drinking
Wine: Malcolm Kushner
Signs You're A Little Too Fond of Wine: Malcolm Kushner

CHAPTER 2

All Purpose Remarks About Wine: These are inspired and
adapted from a June 1993 discussion of funny wine snob
remarks in the Internet newsgroup, rec.food.drink and a
Cron Job column (#5) by Todd Kerpelman at
www.kerp.net/cronjob/cron5.
Pick Up Lines & Responses: These appear all over the
Internet
Wines & Waiters: Malcolm Kushner
Wine Waiter Full Deckisms: Malcolm Kushner
Biggest Lies About Wine: Malcolm Kushner
Clues That A Restaurant Doesn't Specialize in Wine:
Malcolm Kushner

CHAPTER 3

The Wine Virgin: Adapted from an old joke
Why Champagne Is Better Than a Man: Adapted from a
bit that appears all over the Internet

CHAPTER 4
Six Signs You've Had Too Much: Malcolm Kushner
New Wine Warning Labels: Adapted from a bit that
appears all over the Internet
Tasting Room Trouble Shooting Guide: adapted from a bit
that appears all over the Internet
Drunk Test: Malcolm Kushner

CHAPTER 5
French Primer for Wine Students: Malcolm Kushner
Wine Words That Should Exist But Don't: Malcolm
Kushner

CHAPTER 6
Stop The Music: From The Little Brown Book of Anecdotes by
Clifton Fadiman (Little Brown, 1985), p. 75.
Scoring With Wine: Malcolm Kushner
If Famous Authors and Comedians Wrote About Wine:
Malcolm Kushner
Wine Tasting Phrase Creator: Malcolm Kushner
The New "Non-Pretentious" Pretentiousness: Malcolm
Kushner

CHAPTER 7
The Business Success Wine Seminar: Malcolm Kushner
Wine Do's and Don'ts: Malcolm Kushner
Politically Correct Wine Terms: Malcolm Kushner

CHAPTER 8
May You: Malcolm Kushner
To: Malcolm Kushner
Rhyming Toasts: Malcolm Kushner except for last toast -
- an old drinking poem
Heaven Forbid: Malcolm Kushner

CHAPTER 9
Wilde About Champagne:quoted from http://mark-squires.com/quote.html
Fun Facts About Champagne: Facts came from www.zip-pertubing.com; www.funwithwine.com; www.oster.com; www.martini.com; www.champagnemagic.com; www.martiniplace.com; www.cigaraficionado.com; www.bondmovies.com

CHAPTER 10
Wine Lessons: Malcolm Kushner
Clues You're Buying Wine at the Wrong Store: Malcolm Kushner

CHAPTER 11
It's the Law — Really: Laws came from www.smalloak.com; www.dumblaws.com; www.pots-dam.edu

CHAPTER 12
Four Facts About Food, Wine & Health: This appears all over the Internet.
Why Wine Drinkers Are Healthier Than Beer Drinkers: Malcolm Kushner

CHAPTER 13
Herd Mentality: Malcolm Kushner
Investment Advice: Adapted from a bit that appears all over the Internet Wine Trivia Quiz: Trivia came from www.phobialist.com; www.about.com; www.soawanna.com; www.laboheme.com; www.vineswinger.com; www.mangiarebene.net; www.winegirls.com; www.wineloverspage.com; www.beckmanwine.com

Humor Index

Humor Index

Humor Index

ABOUT THE AUTHOR

Malcolm Kushner, "America's Favorite Humor Consultant," is an internationally acclaimed expert on humor and communication. A co-creator of the humor exhibit at The Ronald Reagan Presidential Library, Kushner is also the author of *The Light Touch: How to Use Humor for Business Success* (Simon & Schuster) and *Public Speaking for Dummies* (IDG Books). His audiocassette series *Leading With Laughter*, which documents the humor of six U.S. presidents, has received rave reviews.

Kushner has been profiled in *Time Magazine*, *USA Today*, *The New York Times*, and *The Washington Post*. His television and radio appearances include CNN, C-SPAN, National Public Radio, CNBC, "Voice of America," and "The Larry King Show." *The Wall Street Journal* has called him "Irrepressible."

A popular speaker at corporate and association meetings, Kushner has keynoted everywhere from The Smithsonian Institution to the Inc. 500 Conference. He is based in Santa Cruz, one of California's premiere wine-growing regions.

Visit his web site at www.kushnergroup.com.

He can be reached at mk@kushnergroup.com, or at:
Malcolm Kushner & Associates
P.O. Box 7509
Santa Cruz, CA 95061
831-425-4839

Leading With Laughter®

How U.S. Presidents Use Humor to Relate, Motivate and
Communicate And How You Can Too!

The Program

Powerful humor techniques are explained and illustrated with rare
video clips of U.S. presidents using humor intentionally and success-
fully. Watch Ronald Reagan defuse a tough question with humor.
Hear Richard Nixon create rapport with laughter. Watch Jimmy Carter
score points by poking fun at himself. The program is non partisan
and includes Presidents Kennedy through Clinton.

You'll learn

- Simple humor techniques that let you sparkle without telling jokes
- The secret of not "bombing"
- How to grab attention with humor
- How to build goodwill
- How to turn your sense of humor into a powerful asset
- And much, much more

The Speaker

Malcolm Kushner, "America's Favorite Humor Consultant,"
has performed this program for numerous corporations, associations
and leadership institutes, as well as The Ronald Reagan Presidential
Library and The Smithsonian Institution.

More Info

Contact Malcolm Kushner
Tel 831-425-4839
mk@kushnergroup.com

Please include payment with orders. Send indicated titles to:

Name: _____

Address: _____

City: _____ State: _____ Zip: _____

Phone: _____

Fax: _____

Email: _____

BOOK TITLES	UNIT PRICE	QTY	SUB-TOTAL
Vintage Humor For Wine Lovers (Kushner & Associates, 2002) tradepaper, 160 pp.	9.95	_____	_____
The Light Touch: How to Use Humor For Business Success (Simon & Schuster, 1990) hardcover, 270 pp.	18.95	_____	_____
Leading With Laughter: How U.S. Presidents Use Humor to Relate, Motivate and Communicate (Kushner & Associates, 2001) Six audiocassettes approximately one hour each for Kennedy, Johnson, Ford, Carter, Reagan, Bush	49.95	_____	_____

Add $3.00 for shipping & handling for first book
or audio and $1.00 for each additional product.   _____

CA residents please add 8% sales tax,   _____

TOTAL ENCLOSED: $_____

Please make check payable to Malcolm Kushner.

Send this order form and payment to Malcolm Kushner & Associates
P.O. Box 7509
Santa Cruz, CA 95061
Phone: 831-425-4839
Fax: 831-471-9451
Email: mk@kushnergroup.com

Call for information on discounts for large orders.